text by Enrico Ercole
illustrations by Marisa Vestita

Living in Harmony with Your Cat

WHITE STAR PUBLISHERS

Contents

1.
Choosing the Right Cat

Deciding to live with a cat is an important step that should never be taken lightly. Too often we hear that this animal is less of a commitment because "it doesn't get attached to the owner but to the house" or because "it poops and pees in the litter box and does not need to be taken for a walk." Nothing is farther from the truth. The cat is an animal that needs a deep and symbiotic relationship with the environment that surrounds it, especially with the human members of its family group. Just because they don't come to greet you when you come home (a behavior that is actually characteristic of many felines) does not mean that they don't need your company. Living with a cat means learning to understand the language and mechanisms that rule its social interactions. This means learning to reason like a cat, because your little friend will interact with you exactly as it would with another animal of its species. This is not easy, but it must be done. If you learn to understand it, your life with a feline will bring you a lot of joy. The first question an aspiring "owner" (with a cat the quotation marks are always a must) must ask him/herself is "do I have enough time to

dedicate to the pet?" Although it's true that a cat does not need to be taken for walks, it still needs at least two hours of your company a day. It needs to play with you and receive a good dose of petting.
Then there is bedtime, which it will want to spend with you at all costs. It's not a prescription: the two hours can be distributed as you prefer but they must be as regular as possible because the cat is a very, very habitual animal. Hence, you can leave it alone in the house the whole day (as cats rest for an average of eight hours every twelve) but you should never ignore its requests for attention when you get back. This is even truer for purebred, long or semi-long haired cats, who also need a brushing and occasional cleaning of the eyes and ears.

Debunking a myth: the cat does not get attached only to the home. It develops habits linked to the domestic environment but also becomes strongly attached to people.

The second point to take into careful consideration is how willing you are to share a house with an animal that is not as trainable as a dog. In short, those getting ready to take in a cat should not expect a decisive "no!" to be sufficient to prevent the animal from jumping on the good armchair in the living room or on the shelf housing crystal glassware inherited from grandma when they are out. Although the cat is an easily educated animal of great intelligence, it is not trainable in the usual sense of the word and life with it will always be full of challenges and even some mischief. The same can be said about cat hair on clothes: at regular intervals, the cat will lose a lot of fur due to changes in temperature hence, leaving a sweater on the bed could prove a "fatal" mistake.

Then, there is the question of hygiene, which should never be underrated. The cat is a very clean animal that does most of its own cleaning. However, if it is not possible to let it go outside, there will be the litter box to clean: although certainly not a big deal, it is nonetheless a task that must be performed daily for your animal's as well as your own wellbeing. It should not be forgotten that a dirty litter box harbors infections and germs that are a danger to all!

The financial factor is no less important: the arrival of a cat will be felt in the family budget. It is unthinkable

to plan on feeding the cat leftovers and it is absolutely unacceptable to save by eliminating veterinary visits. Aside from yearly checkups and routine vaccinations, the veterinarian is needed in case of emergencies including illnesses, injuries or infections that a cat can acquire even in the cleanest and most peaceful of environments. Once it is old, after its eighth birthday, it is sure to need some additional healthcare, as it is sure to develop some of the typical age-related conditions, ranging from decline in kidney function to joint problems. And then there is the cat food, which should always be of good quality and varied in flavors: extremely important for keeping the home's pet in good health.

Having considered all of these factors, it should be remembered that living with a cat is a unique experience, rich in rewards. First off, it is the perfect animal for those in search of a companion who is discreet but always present: even cats with the most affectionate dispositions will need long periods to dedicate to sleep or coat cleaning during which they will gladly remain by your side but will not make their presence felt or follow you around as a puppy would.

Then, there are the moments of play, which are extremely important for establishing a good relationship and building mutual trust, especially when the cat is young. And finally some time dedicated to petting, which can be very relaxing not just for the cat but also for you. Sinking your hand into the soft coat and listening to the loud purring, which transmits peace and serenity, can even relieve the stress accumulated during the most horrible of days. Every year newspapers across the world publish articles about how relaxing it is to have a cat by your side, even at work. This is no accident. According to a long-term study conducted at the University of Indiana in the US, watching a video online with cats as protagonists, which always receives record numbers of "likes" on social networks, improves the mood of workers and hence their productivity. In 2015, the Cat Protection League published a rigorous study completed in collaboration with the Mental Health Foundation, which evaluated the extent to which the purring of a cat can relax a person. After all, the cat uses purring to calm itself down and "lull" itself to sleep. It is so effective that a cat will even purr loudly before death.

What's Better, a Purebred or a Mixed Breed?

Once all the aspects, including the future responsibilities and rewards of adopting a cat, have been considered carefully, all that remains is to take your time and choose your companion. The first step in this process should obviously involve the entire family. If no one in the household is affected by allergies or ailurophobia (i.e. fear of cats), then you can proceed to the second step: choosing between a purebred and a mixed breed cat. Here, things get a bit complicated because we cross into the personal sphere, in which it is difficult, if not useless, to offer too many suggestions. Although adopting a cat found on the street or taken from the cat shelter is an act

Not all cats are equal. Choosing between shorthaired and longhaired, purebred and mixed breed cats means a precise choice that should be made responsibly.

of great civil responsibility, one should not feel guilty being particularly attracted by a purebred cat. This desire is perfectly normal and legitimate. The latter need a home as much as the former but thanks to unique physical characteristics (coat length, body shape, character) may suit your needs better. What should be kept in mind is that these cats, whether purebred or mixed breed, will live by your side for the next 8-10 years, sharing the holidays, happy times and sad times with you. Choosing a purebred cat may prove particularly right if one is searching for a companion with certain personality: with rare exceptions, every breed has a quite characteristic disposition. The choices are many: from the mellow Persian to the petulant Siamese; from the rebellious Siberian to the sweet Sphynx; from the reserved Chartreux to the cuddly Ragdoll. It goes without saying that the temperamental ambiguity of the mixed breed must be accepted without reserve, as they may as easily turn out to be an affectionate cat always ready to cuddle as an uncontrollable tornado.

The choice is very important. If you turn to a breeder for a purebred kitten, you must keep your eyes open and take some precautions. Once the desired breed has been chosen, you must organize a reconnaissance tour of all the breeders in your area

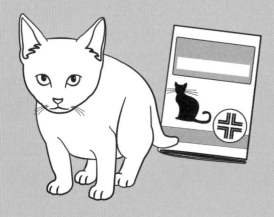

to get a general picture and make a better comparison of the most basic factors such as cleanliness of the areas where the animals are kept and the willingness with which the breeders provide information. After having chosen the breeder you consider the most trustworthy, and most importantly the kitten that has won you over at first sight, but before purchasing, you must request documentation certifying the health of the cat, i.e., papers certifying that the first cycle of vaccinations and any relevant booster shots have been performed. If the feline belongs to a breed that is subject to genetic diseases, you can request the presence of a trusted veterinarian at the time of pick-up, who can personally examine the kitten as well as perform blood, urine and feces exams. A purebred cat can cost as much as several thousand dollars and you have every right to make sure that it is healthy. If it is not possible to have a veterinarian present at the time of purchase, it is recommended you draw up a simple private agreement with the breeder establishing a minimum period within which you will perform all

the relevant health checks. The pedigree, i.e. the document certifying that the cat is of the breed stated and meets all the relevant standards, must be supplied at the time of purchase. The so-called "change of ownership", which must always be provided by the breeder, on the other hand, attests the actual ownership of the cat: it is an essential document for those who want to participate in cat shows. If on the other hand the new arrival is a stray cat that was found on the street, you should take it immediately to the vet's office. The veterinarian will assess its state of health and if necessary, deworm it with medication and give it the first cycle of vaccinations required by law. If you purchase the

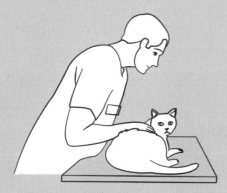

kitten in a store, the same rules apply: documentation must be provided and should include a registration application, a purchase contract, medical records and other materials, depending on the store.

If you find a cat on the street, there are a few fundamental things you can do to make sure the animal is healthy. First of all, it is very important to examine the eyes, nose and mouth: in a healthy cat the mucous membranes should be pink, with no swelling or suspect redness and never too dry or dripping. The corners of the eyes, for example, must be clean; although the presence of some dark organic material is absolutely normal, yellowing of the fur between the eye and the nasal bridge may indicate possible active or recent infections. The coat is another indicator to keep in mind: when stroked (even the wrong way), it should be shiny, clean and with no bad odors (a sick cat stops cleaning itself), and distributed evenly across the entire body with no patching (symptom of dermatitis or infectious diseases). For kittens in particular, a tactile examination of the abdomen can be helpful: the belly should not be too swollen or rigid and tapping

should not cause pain manifested in sudden jerking or loud crying. If you live with people allergic to cats, it's important to know that you are not condemned to a life without cats. In contrast to what is often said, cat allergies are not triggered by fur but by the Fel d1 protein contained in the animal's saliva. Once the saliva deposited on the animals fur during its daily licking sessions dries, it gets released into the air and triggers an at-times violent reaction (including redness and problems breathing) in susceptible subjects when it comes in contact with the mucous membranes of the eyes and nose, or with the lungs if inhaled. Hence, the fur itself has nothing to do with it and choosing the Sphynx, a hairless cat, is not the right solution. What can be a good solution is choosing a Siberian, a breed whose saliva has minimal amounts of the Fel d1 protein. Hence, many people who are allergic to cats have successfully solved their problem by turning to a kitten with a thick coat! Thanks to great advancements in genetics, many breeders are now trying to obtain mixed breeds that can generate "hypoallergenic" individuals of other breeds as well.

The Problems
of Sex

After having chosen the breed, size and color that fits best with your needs and satisfies your personal tastes, you need to address with just as much care the subject of sex. Between male and female cats, there are differences that should not be taken lightly. Most important of these is spraying.

If you choose a male and do not intend to neuter it, a choice that should be discussed with the veterinarian and should be driven solely by the type of life you wish for your cat and not by ethical questions, you will have to deal with the strong smell emitted by urine it will spray on walls and furniture as a signal to nearby females and to mark territory. Not to mention a certain degree of restlessness during mating season. An unneutered male can scent the odor and the call

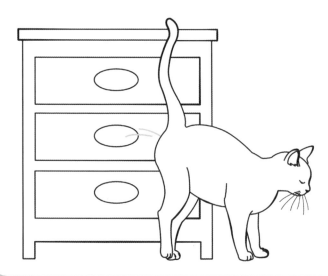

Neutering or spaying a cat should not be thought of as a cruelty but as a preventative treatment and a responsibility.

of a female in heat up to a kilometer away and will do all he can to "communicate" with her and to mate.

If the cat in question is allowed to roam the rooftops and yards, it is almost certain to get involved in violent confrontations with other felines, some of which may be strays, with the risk of being seriously injured or straying too far from home.

On the other hand, if you are looking for an affectionate animal that loves to cuddle, it is best to opt for a neutered male because they tend to acquire more of a "mother's boy" disposition as adults compared to females, who are always more independent, even when spayed.

That which is more crudely called castration can be performed in two ways. Orchiectomy is the removal of the testicles, which produce both the sperm and the hormones responsible for the male's behavior. Performed under short-term, general anesthesia, it is very simple and ensures a quick and painless recovery. Vasectomy is the severing of the conduits along which sperm travel from the testicles outside the body, resulting in the inability to produce offspring during coupling. It does not eliminate any of the undesirable behaviors linked to male hormones, including the unpleasant odor of urine sprayed to mark territory.

Unspayed females produce less problems but while

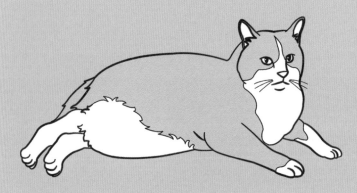

in heat, they will be particularly "insistent". Just like males, females can also undergo different types of spaying procedures. Ovariectomy is the removal of only the ovaries. It is a practical solution because it can be performed at any time, even after several heat cycles or after birthing with no particular problems. Ovariohysterectomy is the removal of the uterus and ovaries. It is only performed in special cases. Tubal ligation, on the other hand, will mean that the cat will still go in heat but not have kittens. Today, it is highly discouraged due to increased probability of developing circulatory problems, and mammary and uterine tumors.

For all these reasons, it is important to talk to a veterinarian before deciding whether to neuter or spay, in order to avoid falling into the trap of thinking of the procedure as a mutilation. To this purpose, you must make the effort to see that a "whole" male cat left closed in a sixth floor apartment with no possibility of satisfying its instinctive needs, will suffer a lot more than a cat that was castrated at a young age. The same can be said for females, for whom it is particularly important to perform the surgery before puberty in order to avoid the development of uterine and ovarian tumors.

The only disadvantage concerns the cat's diet once it becomes an adult: spayed and neutered cats tend to gain weight due to the unavoidable hormonal imbalance resulting from the procedure and the subsequent lack of physical activity. If the weight gain becomes excessive, it is best to consult a veterinarian to decide on a suitably balanced diet.

But how can one tell the difference between a male and a female at first glance? This question may seem trivial but it actually isn't. In an adult cat, it is enough to look for the presence of testicles under the tail, but for kittens younger than 6 months the difference is less obvious since the reproductive system is not yet developed. The secret lies in the distance between the anal and the genital openings: if the two are separated by a certain distance, it's a male; if they are close together, it's a female.

If you don't have the opportunity to examine the private parts of the cat, the shape of the head can serve as an indication: in males, especially in some breeds such as the Chartreux and the British Shorthair, the cheeks are much rounder, giving the head a more massive, squared appearance.

When There is a Child in the House

Cats and children: an eternal dilemma. The problem is as simple as it is important. Children, especially when very small, under three years of age, can mistake the domestic animal for a game, a stuffed toy. They may not realize that it is a living being that can feel pain if its tail or ears are pulled too brusquely. While some dogs are perfectly able to distinguish playful from violent behavior and can put up with a lot during play, cats are decisively less tolerant. For this reason, leaving a toddler alone with a cat is highly inadvisable. Nevertheless, the belief that cats are incompatible with families with small children is completely unfounded: in the past, it was even believed that cats entered children's cribs at night in order to suffocate them by napping on top of them. Today, we know that

any interest that a cat may show in the baby is due to their attraction to the odor of milk that a child might give off, especially after nursing, or the softness of his/her blankets. However, they may become quite "jealous" of the new arrival, who will inevitably impact the attention they receive from the owner. For this reason, you need to pet it and allow it to stay nearby even when you have the child in your arms. In this way, you will avoid the cat starting to see the baby as a rival. With older children, cats can live in complete harmony, but it is just as important to explain to the "human cubs" that it's a very particular animal that is not like the neighbor's dog and that its games are different. Throwing a ball to a cat and expecting it to fetch can prove rather disappointing. In fact, playing with a cat is not easy: playtime for a cat revolves around the simulation of a hunt with behaviors than can often turn unintentionally aggressive and result in scratches and bites. The secret to having fun with a cat is to stop the play session as soon as we see its behavior becoming too aggressive. Signs of aggression can be noted by observing the cat's ears and whiskers: if the former are pulled back and the latter are pushed forward, it means that the cat is preparing a full-blown ambush. At this point, all you have to do is retreat calmly without making any sudden movements and throw it a ball. Objects made of wood or plastic that make noise when they hit the home's walls and baseboards are the best choice: the cat will love them! The shape of the toy is unimportant because the cat will never confuse an inanimate object without a heartbeat with a real mouse, not even if it has whiskers, pink ears and a gray coat!

2.
The
Kitten's
Arrival

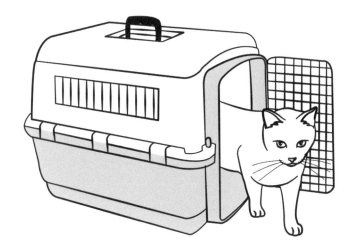

The arrival of a kitten is a fantastic event destined to change the lives of all the family members. From the very first day, your house will no longer be the same: new rules, new presences and new hours will have to be set to make the life of the new arrival (as well as yours) better.

What you have to do when you bring a kitten to your house for the first time is give it some time to get used to the new setting in peace, without forcing it to do something it does not want. A new house for a cat is a real puzzle to solve, with odors to decipher, noises to study and spaces to explore. Hence, it is recommended you open the carrier door and allow the cat to take its time and come out when it is ready, perhaps leaving it closed in a room with the TV off: a cat exploring a new space is very tense and a sudden freight may result in phobias that will be difficult to overcome later on. Therefore, during the first day, it is best to keep the cat in a closed room with bowls of water and food as well as a litter box. It is very important to allow it access to the carrier in which it was brought home, in case it wants to use it as 'a temporary shelter: in a completely new setting, this small space will be the only spot with a familiar smell. After the first day and the first night, the cat will begin to feel more comfortable and start exploring the other rooms of the house. Initially, the kitchen and the bathroom should be kept off limits because they are filled with too many strong odors (food, trash can, cleaning products) and scary sounds (washing machine, dishwasher). The kitten can meet these "monsters" later, when it has gained more confidence.

If you must leave it alone during the day, it may help to place a piece of clothing impregnated with your smell with a ticking clock hidden beneath inside its carrier or near the corner it has claimed as its own (it is perfectly fine if the kitten keeps hiding

A kitten is like a child: it needs us and our guidance to learn what's right and what's wrong.

under the bed, in the carrier or in a dark corner). The ticking clock will remind it of its mother's heartbeat, comforting it.

After four or five days, the kitten should feel comfortable in all the rooms of the house: this is the time to show it where it can find all that it will need in the months to come. The bowls and the litter box will have to be set in locations where we intend to keep them here on out. Cats are very habitual animals and don't like changes and moves, especially when it comes to food and the litter box. Initially, before the kitten has really understood where the litter box is, it may leave some excrements around the house. Just give it some time.

Another factor not to let slide is playtime, which is extremely important as the cat needs it to learn how to interact with its surroundings and as a distraction to any fears it may have. From the very beginning, you can use a wooden ball which makes noise when it hits furniture and walls to help it feel less lonely and keep it from getting bored and "depressed": if it was in the company of its mother and siblings until a short time ago, it will inevitably miss them. It is best to acquire or adopt kittens that are two to three months old; younger cats still need their mother or special care to survive.

House Training

From the very beginning, the cat has to be taught to respect some rules of hygiene. The first task is to get it to use the litter box: this will not take long because cats instinctively look for an area where the ground is very soft, making it easier to bury their excrements and urine. This is an innate habit that in nature permits the cat to erase the traces of its passage. Hence, it is deeply rooted in every cat from a young age, manifesting itself as early as the third-fourth week after birth (they only gain full control of the sphincter in the second week of life).

The secret lies in the how the litter box is "introduced" to the kitten. Once you have decided where the litter box will be, you must show it to the cat: it will carefully inspect it, smelling it and digging some practice

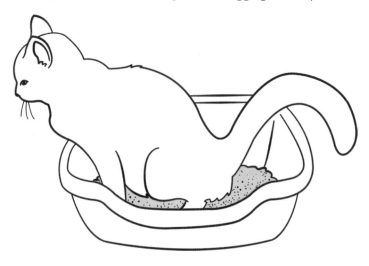

holes. If this is not enough and excrements are still being left around the house (initially, a few exceptions should be made), it will suffice to place the kitten next to its "mess", without raising your voice or scolding it, and then take it immediately to its litter box. It may take a bit of time, but the association will soon become clear.

If, on the other hand, the cat continues to defecate outside the litter box, you must try to identify the reason behind this behavior. It may be physiological, in which case the kitten does not have enough time to get to the litter box after having felt the stimulus, or psychological. In the case of the latter, you must carefully consider some factors: maybe the litter box is in a location that is not suitable due to an unpleasant noise or odor. If so, it should be moved. For example, some owners tend to place the litter box on the balcony without considering traffic noise, which can deter the cat from using it. It may seem like an exaggeration, but this is not so. It should be kept in mind that a cat hears noises that we are not capable of perceiving. On the other hand, if you have a back yard and the cat is free to go out, it will take care of its bathroom needs on its own, choosing the spot that suits it most. If you don't want the cat to leave you "mementos" underneath the rose bushes, especially since cat urine is not exactly a cure-all for plants, you can create a spot for it to use by loosening soil or adding sand to an area that you prefer: the cat will choose it on its own as it will provide the perfect covering material. However, don't be fooled into thinking that an outdoor cat does not need a litter box: many cats still prefer to come back home to use the litter box or to use a litter box prudently placed in the back yard.

The Correct Diet

For kittens, a proper diet during the first months of life is extremely important for correct development and a healthy growth. Therefore, it is fundamental to know what to do and the steps that must be followed, especially if you find yourself taking care of a kitten that is not yet self-sufficient. During the first four or five weeks of life, kittens are nourished by the mother, who nurses them. During this period, nourished with the so-called "first milk" (colostrum), the kittens will grow at impressive rates, gaining 5 to 10 per cent of their bodyweight per day. In the

The health of a kitten does not depend solely on being vaccinated, but also on a balanced diet suitable to its age.

fourth week, the so-called "weaning", i.e. the gradual introduction of solid food, can begin. You can start with a few teaspoons of cat formula (there are various brands available on the market), dissolving some dry food or small quantities of meat or fish-based baby food in it.

Once fully weaned, between the seventh and eighth week of life, the kitten must start eating solid foods: there are many excellent quality cat foods available on the market calibrated for the caloric and nutritional needs of a growing cat. During this stage, it is very important not to think about saving and to purchase only good quality foods, best if recommended by a veterinarian, to ensure the cat does not develop a deficiency caused by an unbalanced diet. The first meals can be given by mixing a little bit of solid food with some warm water or milk to make them more appetizing. Successively, you can transition to just cat food for kittens (meat or fish flavored) mixed with some overcooked rice if you wish (but keep an eye out for intolerances). The number of meals will progressively decrease from four/five in the second month to four in the third month and finally to two, more substantial meals a day in the sixth month. Feeding a kitten little but often helps get its body used to

the correct absorption of nutrients without tiring out a still developing digestive system. It is also very important for it to always have fresh and clean water available. Even after the cat's permanent teeth come in, its daily nutritional needs will remain the same until a year of age.

At this point, it is best to bring up a topic that is very important, especially during this growth stage: it is crucial to debunk the belief that food prepared at home is healthier than the food produced industrially. Nothing is farther from the truth. Preparing a balanced meal for a cat, especially for a cat that's still growing, is very complicated because it must provide the animal with the correct amount of calories, and the right amount of taurine and other essential substances. In fact, the perfect meal for a growing cat must consist of 50 per cent beef or white meat cut into small pieces, raw or lightly seared, 25 per cent cooked and well drained (to eliminate excess starch) rice or pasta and 25 per cent vegetables (carrots, zucchini and green leaf vegetables are ideal). In addition, you have to ensure that the meat contains the right amount of taurine, an absolutely essential substance for a cat. A deficiency in this substance can lead to serious health problems, especially in cats that are still growing. This is why purchasing industrially produced food, which is now produced to extremely high quality standards, is best.

The kitten should be accustomed to a diet that includes both wet and dry food immediately. The latter has undeniable advantages: it can be given anywhere without making a mess, it does not need to be refrigerated, it is a concentrate of nutrients, it is needed in smaller quantities, it's cheaper and it helps keep the cat's teeth clean and strong. However, it cannot be the only type of food in your cat's diet.

How do you know that you are doing the right thing? It's easy: always consult the veterinarian if you have any doubts and keep an eye on the kittens weight. In the first weeks, kittens gain on average 10-30 grams (0.3-1 oz), although these numbers change with the breed.

Living with
Other Animals

Generally, cats don't like sharing their spaces. However, living with other animal species or cats is possible, and sometimes desirable and even recommended to avoid solitude-related depression, if it is managed properly. The most important thing is to act sensibly and to try your best to put yourself in your cat's "paws", to reason like a cat. To this purpose, it helps to know that for a cat, another animal is either a possible prey to chase or a predator from which to escape, while another feline may be a rival from whom to defend its territory, a partner with whom to reproduce or simply another member of the cat colony to tolerate. Once this

The cat is an animal that can live with other animal species, dogs included. However, keep in mind that it is still one of nature's most skilled hunters.

is understood, you are ready to choose a new companion for yourself and your cat.

With a few exceptions, animals that live in cages, aquariums or terrariums are small and hence, represent possible prey to a cat. Living with them may prove complicated if not plain dangerous. Cases of cute games between a cat and a guinea pig, rabbit or mouse are no rarity; however, it would be a fatal error to leave the room while they are taking place. Playing is an important part of a cat's life, but we should never forget that in addition to being an entertaining activity, as it is for humans, it constitutes real hunting practice and hence, at the moment of greatest excitement, instinct may take over with disastrous results. Therefore, it is highly inadvisable leaving a cat and a hamster or guinea pig out and about on their own. Just as it is inadvisable to leave the cat alone with an iguana or any other large reptile, which may bite, triggering a sudden and violent response. The same can be said about birds, which in flight represent an irresistible attraction as well as a delicious meal. Even fish can prove to be a dangerous companion because cats often develop an insane habit of drinking water from open aquariums and fish bowls: although of little danger to the fish, which they are unlikely to succeed in catching, this

is a harmful behavior because of the substances that may be dissolved in the water, above all fish food. Things can also become complicated if a cat must live with a dog. If the two grow up together, problems are highly unlikely. On the contrary, they are almost certain to become inseparable friends. However, if the dog is an adult and the cat is still young, you must proceed with caution to avoid triggering phobias in the little feline that will accompany it into adulthood. Since at the sight of the cat, the dog will want to sniff and "play" with it, jumping around and wagging its tail, in other words behaving in a way that is certain to frighten the kitten, it is important that the two first get used to each other's odors without coming into direct contact. Keeping them in two adjacent rooms with the door closed for a few days can be a good start. Placing a blanket impregnated with the smell of one into the room of the other can also produce good results. The actual introduction will have to be strictly supervised, with the dog kept on a leash and the cat free to move around.

Never hold the cat in your arms; this will make it feel imprisoned. Some time will be needed before the cat stops hissing at the dog, maybe even a few months, but eventually the two will learn to understand each other. The greatest obstacles to their communication, especially in the beginning, are differences in body language such as that of the tail, which is agitated by the dog when it is excited or happy, and by the cat when it is nervous.

If on the other hand, the new roommate is another cat, you need to keep in mind that unlike a dog, which is a social animal used to being part of a pack into which new members may be admitted, the cat is an animal that is solitary and territorial. Therefore, it is possible that it will feel its territory being threatened by the other animal. Hence, the introduction of a kitten into a house with an adult cat already in residence should be managed with care: don't rush things, give the two roommates time to establish their territories. A few disputes are inevitable but with time their relationship will get better.

Can They be Educated?

Educating a cat is difficult but not impossible. Certainly, you will not be able to train it as you would a dog, but you can still teach it some rules to make living together easier. The first step towards good education is choosing the right name: if you want your cat to respond to your call, avoid giving imaginative names, opting for something more basic but effective instead. The best names are those composed of one or two syllables with ringing vowels. It is decidedly more likely that a cat will respond to a name like Max, Simba or Jack rather than Garfield or Mr. Bigglesworth. Since name recognition is a process that can be effectively

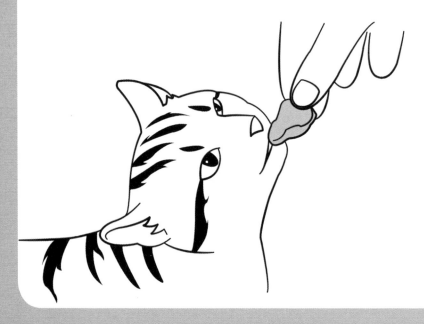

Educating (not training, mind you) a cat is possible, but only if you understand and respect how it thinks.

triggered in some cats but remain inactive in others, to ensure the animal learns to associate the sound with itself, it is very important to start working on it when it's still a kitten by creating an association between a treat and every positive response. A treat given every time the name is pronounced will give the sound positive value, setting off a cognitive process that will serve to draw the cat's attention to the call. Obviously, you can't expect this to work immediately and every time, but by doing this you will ensure a solid foundation on which to build further education. Since it is impossible to expect the cat to understand what is right and what is wrong on its own, you must teach it from an early age what it can and cannot do, where it can and cannot stay, what it can and cannot eat and what it can and cannot use as a scratching post. How? Certainly not by hitting it: a smack will never "register" as a punishment but rather as a challenge or, even worse, as a game. The only way to teach a cat what it cannot do is to catch it in the act and to reprimand it by loudly saying NO or its name, or by making a loud noise (clapping of the hands or a slap of the newspaper). A sudden noise will disrupt the concentration needed by the cat to perform a certain action. It may take some

time, but eventually it will give up jumping on the shelf filled with knick-knacks, sleeping in the bidet or strolling on the table set for a meal. It is very important that the reprimand is given at the time of mischief, because if given after the fact, the miscreant will not associate the reprimand with the action for which it's intended. The often recommended "water spraying" method should be avoided at all costs: the only outcome achieved by spraying a misbehaving cat with water is an association between your presence and a punishment that is so loathsome that you risk triggering rejection behaviors directed towards you that will prove far from pleasant.

All of this will prove effective only and exclusively if you have first gained the cat's trust and respect by making your role in the family group clear. To do this, you must activate learning processes that in cats are manifested mainly during play, which consists not so much of ball chasing, but of full contact play. Playing with a cat, especially if it is still young or a kitten, means teaching it not to cross forbidden lines. It is very common for a cat to get carried away while playing and bite down rather

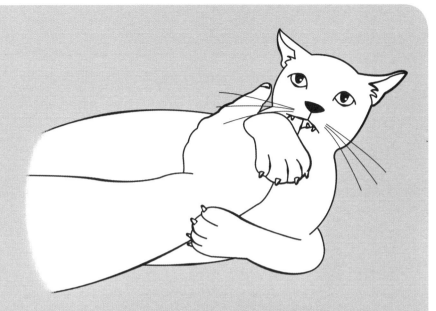

hard or painfully scratch hands and arms: when this happens, the game should stop completely. Any type of punishment other than immediate abandonment of the "battle field", especially slaps, will not be taken as a reprimand but only and exclusively as an incitement to continue.

To make this mechanism even more effective, you can try some real educating: play with the cat, allowing it to nibble and squeeze your hand, and when you feel the play getting too aggressive, reprimand the cat in a dry, authoritarian tone. If it shows to have understood you by loosening its hold or retracting its claws, than you can reward it with a tasty treat and affection. If on the other hand the cat continues to be excessively aggressive, you should ignore it for at least half an hour and then try again later.

Disease Prevention

A kitten, regardless of whether it comes from a cat shelter, a pet store, a breeding facility, or the street, must receive regular vaccinations. This will allow it to live a peaceful life and keep away potentially dangerous illnesses and infections.
It is very, very important that the kitten receives its first vaccines at two months, i.e. when the vaccines will no longer interfere with the natural antibodies supplied by breast milk. Experts generally agree that your pet should be vaccinated against such diseases as panleukopenia, feline viral rhinotracheitis, calcivirus and, at the veterinarian's

A proper vaccination plan, annual check-ups and good household hygiene will guarantee your cat a healthy and peaceful life.

discretion, against chlamydophila. These vaccines provide total coverage and require additional shots within 90-100 days and subsequent yearly booster shots. Booster shots are best given a few days early to avoid an excessive drop in antibodies that would leave the cat unprotected. The rabies vaccine is also required by law, and the duration of the immunity it provides depends upon the type of vaccine chosen. Today, there are vaccines available in a number of countries for both feline infectious peritonitis (FIP) and feline immunodeficiency virus (FIV). There is also a vaccine for the equally fearsome feline leukemia virus; however, it is only recommended for individuals living in or coming from a cat shelter or those who have frequent contact with strays.

Disease prevention does not stop with vaccines, it also includes domestic cleanliness: a cat is still rather vulnerable, subject to infections triggered by the presence of fleas and other parasites. Using a good parasite prevention treatment and cleaning their favorite napping spot with flea spray or a jet of steam can help avoid these problems. It should be remembered that fleas can enter the house directly from the outdoors without being transported "on board" a cat.

Cats and Apartments

If you are renting an apartment, the presence of a cat must be allowed by the owner. If the owner does not want animals in the apartment, he must explicitly state so in the rental agreement.

In most States, a cat in an apartment building must always have a collar and a tag bearing your name and telephone number. In some cases, it also must wear a second tag, stating the date of the most recent feline rabies vaccination. This is because if the cat goes outside (although it would be better to fence off balconies and patios with additional netting before the cat's arrival, so it does

In most states, a cat in an apartment building must always have a collar and a tag bearing your name and telephone number.

not go exploring the outside world) you can't follow it, and it's impossible to know where it will go. It may pass from roof to roof or garden to garden and reach your neighbors. A curious or hungry cat, or one in heat, can cover several kilometers! The ID tag will allow anyone to bring it home, as well as locate you if the cat has gotten into trouble. In addition, to help avoid serious inconveniences, its recommended you get an insurance: with a small annual payment, you can avoid serious monetary loss.

In the very unlikely case that your cat is not neutered, another problem that can complicate your relationship with your neighbors is spraying. Any spraying outside your apartment (which cats tend to do in the same spots) may serve as justification for a higher contribution towards stairwell cleaning costs justified by the resulting odor. This is a good reason to maintain an even closer control over your cat.

If you have pets, renting may be difficult in some States, since each has specific laws relating to pets. For example, the State with the most comprehensive set of laws relating to pets is California. Among other aspects, these laws cover the minimum weaning period for kittens, annual veterinary requirements, and the length of time a cat may be impounded. Rhode Island's cat law, on the other

hand, addresses solely the problem of roaming and feral cats. There aren't many States that have no statewide provisions that mention cats by name. These include Hawaii, Idaho, Kentucky, Ohio and Washington. For the most part, State laws deal with rabies vaccination requirements. In some States, domestic animals require licensing at the state or local level. Although all States require some sort of licensing for dogs, the only State to require the licensing of cats is Rhode Island. For example, in Colorado's Control and Pet Licensing provisions, dog licensing requirements are outlined in detail, while cat specific requirements are left to the discretion of individual municipalities. In New Hampshire, local governments are given the power to set cat licensing requirements. Having said that, cat friendly housing is not easy to find. It limits your choices and requires more time, organization and persuasion skills. Start by looking for pet friendly housing in the area you will be moving to and everything else will become easy as pie. Dealing with people who love animals as much as you will eliminate one source of stress during your move. Some great places to

look for references for pet-friendly housing in your new area include local vets, humane societies and animal control. Although, pet-friendly housing is your best bet, it is not always one that is available or possible.

When planning a move, you should first make sure your rental agreement states that you may have a pet. If it does not, make sure that does not explicitly say that you are not allowed to have pets. Don't fall into the trap of thinking you are allowed to have pets because pets are present in the building or on the property, or because someone told you so. The only thing that matters is what is written in your rental agreement. And don't automatically discard an advertisement that says "no pets": bring the matter up with the landlord, he may be open to the possibility under certain conditions.

3.
A Cat-
friendly
House

There is no such thing as a fully cat-friendly home. This is because often there is a real chasm between our aesthetic desires and the practical expectations of our hairy roommate; expectations shaped by daily needs that you would do well to accept if you don't want to lay a foundation for an unequal war. Let us start by saying that a cat is by nature a hunter: this makes it relentlessly curious, a tireless explorer and a cunning hunter. Therefore, there is no corner of the house that will net get explored sooner or later. You can teach the cat to respect some rules, but don't expect to control it, especially when you're not home. Hence, it is best to put your mind at rest by locking all the fragile objects in cabinets and arming yourself with sticky rollers to remove cat hair from carpets and armchairs. For the touchy subject of "doing its nails", you can distract it from the couch or the curtains by providing it with a comfortable scratching post made of twine or a piece of wood: although the cat may initially ignore it, preferring to continue to use walls and furniture, with time it will inevitably choose the materials that give it the most satisfaction. The secret is to pick the cat up and carry it to the scratching post every time you see it sharpening its claws on unwanted objects, without yelling or slapping. If the cat gets fixated with something and refuses to give it up, you can resort to repellant sprays that can be found for sale or to placing a bottle filled with water in front of the "crime scene" (no one knows why but it works).

Another important aspect of living with a cat is rendering the house safe for the feline. The dangers hidden in an apartment are many: from a washing machine left open, a mysterious and irresistible

The "perfect" owner should treat his/her cat as an equal, as any other member of the family. The rules should be few but clear-cut.

chasm that is sure to attract the cat, particularly if it's still young (hence, before putting in your laundry and turning on the machine, check that your cat is not inside), to foods that may have been inadvertently left within paw's reach. Speaking of the latter, the myth that a cat's acute sense of smell permits it to distinguish foods that are dangerous from those that are innocuous is false. Nothing can be farther from the truth! A bag of raisins, just like a bar of chocolate (especially dark chocolate), raw egg whites, garlic or cooked onion may seem appetizing to a cat, but are in fact dangerous to its health because its body cannot tolerate them. Plastic bags can also be dangerous. The noise they make makes them irresistible: however, while playing, a cat may get its head stuck in a handle with the risk of hurting itself or even suffocating. Objects hanging from above can also be a potential danger: if the cat tries to "capture" a plug hanging from a table, it could tip a heavy household appliance on top of itself. Then there is the kitchen: the trash can is a goldmine of magnificent odors and flavorful things to dig through, but also a receptacle of germs and objects that may cause injury or dangerous infections if they come into contact with the delicate mucous membranes of the nose and eyes.

It is hence advisable to use very stable trash cans that are difficult to tip over and open, or to store them in a difficult to access location.

A gas cooktop or, even worse, an induction cooktop can cause serious burns because a cat used to jumping onto furniture may not be able to tell the difference between them and a regular surface. Balconies and window ledges should be treated with equal care since cats love looking outside. Although it's quite unlikely for a cat to leap from a fourth floor balcony of its own free will, it is less improbable for it to fall after being spooked by the window being slammed shut behind it or an unexpected noise.

A little known fact worth some attention is the attraction a cat feels to bleach, which can prove dangerous not only because it is poisonous when ingested (which is unlikely to happen) but also because it is irritating to the mucous membranes of the nose, mouth and eyes.

A safety consideration best extended to other cleaning products as well. Although many of the cleaning products are lemon scented, which makes them "unappetizing" to domestic animals, it should always be kept in mind that they can still be a danger simply by coming in contact with cat paws. Once on paws, they will inevitably be ingested along with hair during grooming, which a cat performs with its tongue.

Play and Hunt Simulation

Playing is very important for the correct psychological and physical development of your cat, also in adulthood, especially if it is not allowed into the garden to work off its hunting instincts. Precisely because it learns to hunt and defend itself from predators during play, you should pay particular attention to what you provide it for such an educational pastime. You can't expect the cat to leave your sewing kit alone if you use a cotton reel during play, to ignore the nut bowl if the walnuts you throw it come from there, or to leave dangling wires alone if you let it play with ribbons and strings tied to the back of chairs. For all of

For cats, playing is none other but a simulation of a hunt. If you play with it by turning yourself into astute prey, fun will be guaranteed to all.

these reasons, it is best to give your cat toys that don't resemble objects that you don't want to draw its attention to. A mouse on a spring or a plastic chicken is not a more effective toy: shape matters little to your cat, as it will never let the shape of an inanimate object (which has no heartbeat) fool it into thinking of it as possible prey. A wooden ball that makes noise when it hits walls and baseboards will be perfect. Even wrestling with its owner will be stimulating to a cat. However, be careful not to overdo it: overcome with excitement, it is not unusual for a cat to seriously bite or scratch. If this happens, saying its name loudly will distract it and make it stop. It is very important not to smack it if you find it running around the house playing with something you don't want it to touch because unexpected aggression will serve only as an additional incentive to play, a sort of challenge, instead of a punishment. The most important thing to do when playing with a cat is to try to think like one. Play for a cat represents a real hunt: hiding a toy and then making it appear out of nowhere will get the maximum reaction! It goes without saying that if you don't want the cat to check out the houseplants, it's best not to have it play with sticks or even worse, leaves.

The "Bed"

Cats pass about 60 per cent of their day sleeping or more precisely, snoozing and resting (real sleep actually takes up a substantially smaller amount of time). This means that the designated place for long naps will be chosen carefully. It will not always be the same because cats love curling up in different spots depending on the environmental conditions at the time, from the surrounding room temperature to the noise level. The three or four spots chosen as the ideal places for a rest will always be preferred to all others: these may include the beautiful basket complete with a blanket that you chose for it, however don't expect

A warm and comfortable spot for a nap is the dream of all cats. However, spending money on wicker baskets or elegant poufs is pointless: the cat will choose its favorite bed on its own.

it to become the only spot. Warm throws, comfortable couches, but also stranger spots, such as the dirty laundry basket and the dark corner of a closet, will always be preferred over the most comfortable cat bed. For this reason, you have to make locations where you don't want the cat to go inaccessible, the bed included. Don't forget, the bed is a highly sought-after resting spot for your cat, especially when you're not at home, because its warm, soft and above all, impregnated with your odor. The hygiene-driven tendency of most owners to not want their cats on the bed is understandable, however a bedspread placed over the comforter during the day can easily resolve the problem of cat hair without starting a conflict with your pet. Take care of the pillows! Some cats love holing up between the pillow and the headboard: if this happens, remove the pillows during the day or cover them with a sheet. A dirty pillow can be very irritating as well as decidedly not hygienic.

In addition, due to its love of warmth, it is not unlikely for the cat to climb under that blanket. Locking it out of the room, especially when you are inside, may prove a very bad idea: there are cats capable of scratching at a door for hours! What must be prevented at all costs on the other hand is the habit that some cats develop of sleeping on radiators, because hot air can dry their mucous membranes potentially leading to serious health problems.

The Back Yard: the Joys and the Dangers

The back yard is a wonderful resource for cat owners, especially those who have to leave the house for many hours. Being able to go outside, through a convenient cat door, guarantees the cat a lot of entertainment and movement. However, in this case as well, you need to make sure it is a cat-friendly environment from which dangers such as wire fencing, deep water-filled basins (especially if you have young cats) and plants harmful to a cat's health are banned. The latter (also indoors) can prove some of a cat's most dangerous traps. Some examples? The extremely common holly produces sweet berries that, if ingested,

A nice back yard with plants and gullies to explore will make any cat happy. Watch out for the dangers, which may truly be many and most unexpected!

even during play, can cause fits of vomiting and diarrhea; the common poinsettia has poisonous leaves; the azalea secretes a sap that can alter the heart rate; jasmine triggers reactions in the nervous system that lead to seizures; hydrangea and oleander can prove extremely toxic; and lily flowers and leaves can cause serious kidney damage even if ingested in small quantities. Other common plants and flowers that can cause problems, above all for the digestive, nervous and cardiac systems, include ivy, poppies, tulips, the Virginia creeper, iris, daffodils, mums, and horse chestnut. Even the water gathering in planter saucers can prove dangerous: cats love drinking dirty water that they come across, but if it contains mosquito eggs or the eggs of other insects, it can have very harmful effects. In addition, any herbicides that you may be using can dissolve in rainwater and end up ingested.

The common grass, on the other hand, has beneficial effects. Cats chew it to help stimulate vomiting, which expels hairballs (also called trichobezoar) accumulated in the stomach following grooming sessions performed by the cat with its tongue. Even the so-called "catnip", more properly called "nepata cataria", can be useful for the soothing effects it has on the cat's body.

4.
Taking
Care
of a Cat

The health of a cat does not depend exclusively on the veterinary care that you are able to provide or on a correct vaccination plan, but also, and above all, on a domestic environment that ensures a healthy and safe life, without obstacles to the cat's daily rituals. A clean and comfortable litter box, clean food bowls and time dedicated to coat care will prevent the development of phobias and refusal behaviors that may degenerate into difficult to treat illnesses in the long run. To prevent this from happening, just act sensibly and follow a few suggestions, and above all observe the behavior of your cat and try to identify any elements present in the house that may disturb it. This may prove difficult because you are dealing with an animal that has extremely acute senses, which permit it to sense sounds, odors and movements that are almost "invisible" to you. To give an example: how annoying can the buzz of a battery charger be to an animal that can hear 4.5 times better than you can? Or, how unpleasant can the odor of trash be to a nose 40 times more sensitive than yours?

The Litter Box

The litter box is an object that must not be neglected if you want life with your cat to remain pleasant. First of all, it should be stated that every house with a cat should have a litter box: sooner or later it will come in handy, even if the animal is used to taking care of its bodily functions in the back yard. It will come in handy when the cat gets older, when it is ill or has difficulty getting around.

The litter box should be set in a comfortable spot that is easy to reach and not exposed to temperatures that are too high or too low. Many choose the bathroom, which, as long as you leave

Cleaning a litter box is by no means a pleasant task, but it is the duty of every "good" cat owner. It will ensure both you and your cat stay healthy!

the door open, is a good choice. However, the loud noise made by the washing machine may scare the cat, giving rise to a reluctance of using the litter box due to fear.

It is difficult to decide on the best model to recommend: today, there are models for all preferences available for sale, including more technological models and covered models with an entry flap and an odor control filter. All work perfectly well as long as the cat can fit inside comfortably while in the sitting position, the position it takes to expel both urine and feces: a Maine Coon or a Ragdoll, for example, may find it difficult to use a covered litter box and hence choose not to use it.

Uncovered litter boxes, consisting of only the tray, are generally preferred by cats because they allow the cat to keep watch on the surrounding environment. However, they leave the feces and urine-soaked litter clumps in plain view, which the owner may find unpleasant. What counts most, beyond the shape, is that the litter box is made of non-toxic materials resistant to scratching and above all, easy to wash. The edges, which should be tall to ensure the cat does not scatter litter all around when it digs to cover its excrements, are very important.

As for the litter itself, the clumping litter brands containing sodium bentonite are a reliable classic although recent studies have shown that they may prove dangerous the animal's health in the long run. Silica gel litter is also a very practical option, because it absorbs liquids and dehydrates feces, preventing bad odors and making cleaning the litter box with a scoop easier. Natural litters on the other hand are composed of biodegradable materials (cellulose, paper, sawdust etc.) that can be flushed down the toilet (unlike other litters that must be thrown out with the trash), but they must be changed more often due to lower absorbency. The only thing that matters is that the particles are fine grained, unscented and not used in excessive quantities.

The feces and the clumps of urine should be removed every day and the litter changed completely at least once a week.

Those who have more than one cat using the same litter box will obviously have to shorten these times, although it would be best to provide a

different litter box for each cat. The litter box should be washed with non-toxic cleaning products without a strong scent every fifteen days. It is important not to use bleach when cleaning not only because it leaves a residual odor that is unpleasant to cats but also because it reacts with compounds contained in urine increasing the unpleasantness and persistence of the odor. If you really want to reduce odors to a minimum, you can clean the litter box with water mixed with a small amount of vinegar. In addition, you can add a thin layer of baking soda to the bottom of the litter box, underneath the litter: this will significantly reduce the smell of urine.

If there are small children living in the house, you have to make sure they don't get too close to the cat's litter box: they may be tempted to play with the sand and come into contact with dangerous bacteria.

The same can be said about small dogs, who may find the litter box convenient for taking care of their own bodily functions, rendering it unpleasant to its legitimate owner.

The Bowls

The eating area is very important to a cat. The bowls must not only be filled with tasty, balanced food but also be placed in a carefully chosen spot in the house. The kitchen is the location most often chosen: this is not wrong but you should make sure to place the bowls in a spot that is far away from the trash can and the stove, to make sure there are no strong odors to disturb the cat during its meal. The balcony is also a good choice, as long as the spot where the bowls are placed is protected from excessive heat and cold. The same holds true for the patio. This will avoid dangerous alteration of food

leftover in the bowls. Excessive cold could freeze the edges of the bowl's contents drastically reducing its appeal, while heat may cause dry food to become rancid faster. In addition, locations that are too open to the elements could increase the number of insects that end up in the wet food or the water. This is why it is highly unadvisable to place bowls of food in the back yard: in addition to insects, and some stray cat passing through who may tuck in, birds are also attracted by the food. Not to mention ants, which will overrun leftovers left both inside and around the bowl. Finally, it is best to make sure that the bowls are not made using perishable or toxic materials, and above all, that they are easy to wash: steel is the best choice because even after numerous washings, it cannot be scratched, and most importantly, it does not retain odors of foods or cleaning products. The bowls should also have low edges, which don't require the cat to eat in an uncomfortable position or with whiskers bent at an excessive angle.

If the chosen bowl does not have a base completely or partially covered with non-slip rubber, it is best placed next to a wall. This will avoid the cat having to chase the bowl every time the feline's vigorous licking shifts it. It is best to have three bowls: one for wet food, one for water, and another, possibly bigger bowl for the dry food. All should be placed on a mat of easily washable rubber that will make cleaning any pieces of food scattered around the bowls easier while acting as a barrier between the food and the floor, which is often washed using cleaning products that may leave traces of unpleasant odors.

Coat
Care

Everyone knows that the cat is a clean animal that is perfectly capable of taking care of its own coat and personal hygiene with no additional help. And it is really good at it, especially if you consider that according to some studies, cats pass 20 per cent of their day doing just that. Nevertheless, semi-long and longhaired cats may require an occasional bath or simply a thorough brushing session, especially when the seasons are changing and a lot of hair is being shed. Generally, this happens twice a year, in correspondence with the greatest temperature shifts. However, today these cycles have been inevitably altered by excessive heating in the winter, especially in homes equipped with radiators, and use of air conditioning in the

Brushing can become a relaxing time for both the cat and the owner as well as help remove excess fur and eliminate tangles.

summer, rendering shedding an almost perennial phenomenon.

When the cat begins to shed, some grooming sessions will help liberate it of loose hair. This minimizes the amount of hair found around the house and reduces the amount of dead hair ingested by the cat. Ingested hair goes on to accumulate in the stomach and is later ejected via the mouth by energetic retching (the so-called hairballs). In addition, regular brushing helps avoid the formation of hair tangles, which may lead not only to the formation of unattractive clumps of fur, but of painful matting.

With the right tools and a little bit of skill grooming will only take half an hour a week. Here is what you must have in the house: a brush (ideal for brushing a long, thick coat; best if it is soft with thin metal teeth or pig bristle), a comb (very helpful for a longhair cat; with coarse and fine teeth or with two rows of teeth, coarse on one side and fine on the other), a grooming mitt (slips onto a hand; has a soft surface covered with small, abrasive semi-spheres that catch loose hair; particularly useful for shorthaired cats), a suede cloth (not indispensable but it can add shine to a cat's coat), and small pieces of sterile gauze (soaked

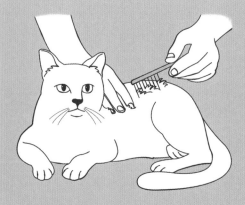

in hydrogen peroxide, they are used to clean the corners of the eyes, especially for white cats whose pure white hair may become permanently stained by tear deposits).

Once you have the necessary tools, you can begin the practical step. It's not complicated: if done gently, a grooming session can even be confused for a petting session, transforming into a pleasant moment of relaxation to spend in the owner's company. First, start by brushing in the direction of hair growth with the coarse comb, looking for knots to untangle. Avoid tugging on the fur or causing pain. If the knots don't come undone immediately, you may have to use your hands or, if the tangle is really bad, a seam ripper from a sewing kit: insert the teeth of the comb between the tangle and the cat's skin, to form a shield, then work your way through the tangle with the seam ripper. When all the tangles have been removed, pass the fine comb through the fur to eliminate all the loose hairs. A few more strokes with a soft brush and the cat's coat will appear magnificently well-groomed, fluffy and clean. Using the grooming

mitt, massage the nose, paws and the area under the tale. Before throwing out the fur trapped in the brush, carefully check to make sure there are no black or whitish specks that may indicate the presence of adult fleas or eggs.

Now let's talk about bath time. Ignoring aesthetic reasons, which are mostly associated with the world of cat shows, a bath should not and must not be considered a necessity, not even for Persian or Angora cats. If a cat lives in a clean environment and is looked after correctly, it will never need a bath. However, some extreme cases may arise. For example, when it returns after an exploration of a dusty basement or a stroll between the oily parts of a car motor, or simply when it gets old and sick and is no longer able to take care of its personal hygiene. If a bath becomes necessary, the most important thing to know is to never point a jet of water directly at a cat. After having filled the bottom of a bathtub with water at 95-98 °F (35-37°C), gently put the cat in, making sure the water does not rise more than half way up its paws, so it feels safe. It is important to never completely let

go of the cat, or it may suddenly jump out of the tub, spraying water everywhere. Once it is relatively calm, soak its back repeatedly by scooping water from the bottom of the tub and pouring it over the cat with a small bowl or by squeezing out a sponge soaked with water. When the cat is completely wet, including its wooly undercoat, apply the shampoo. Purchase the shampoo at a pet store, making sure it is antiseptic and does not leave a strong odor behind. It is important not to use a shampoo intended for human use because it could be toxic to animals, irritate the mucous membranes of the eyes, mouth and nose or produce a lot of foam, requiring you to rinse too many times. Once the entire body and paws (never the nose) are coated in soap, you must rub the dirtier areas well, paying particular attention to the area under the tale of semi-long and longhaired cats. When rinsing, it is very important to remove all remnants of soap.

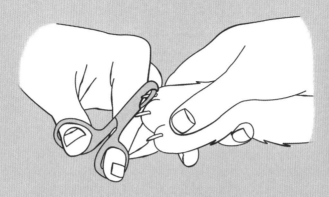

You can use a jet of water at the lowest pressure setting. Hold it close to the cat's body and never direct it at the face.

If the coat is dry and extremely tangled, a conditioner should be applied and left in for a few minutes. During this period, you can wrap the cat in a warm towel creating a beneficial compressional action that will help the conditioner in its regenerative function. To dry the cat, just wrap it in a towel and vigorously rub. Avoid using the hairdryer at all costs, as it is sure to scare the cat.

A nail trim may also be necessary, especially if the cat is an indoor cat. Although this is a very simple procedure, it must be performed with a lot of care, if possible after having seen it done by the veterinarian: set the cat on a stable surface; hug the cat, forcing it to crouch down; while keeping it still, apply light pressure on the pads, forcing the claws to come out. Using a nail trimmer for cats or a small nail clipper, cut away only the transparent tip of the claw: it is extremely important not to cut any further to avoid painfully injuring the quick.

Parasites

To keep your cat healthy, it is very important to protect it from parasites. The most common parasites are fleas, *Ctenocephalides felis*. Small insects about 0.15 inch (4 mm) in length, they are incredibly hardy and prolific, capable of laying as many as 40 eggs a day. The eggs, once hatched, release tiny larvae that fall from the animal's fur and hide throughout the house: in the gaps between tiles, behind the baseboard, in the cracks in the parquet, between the threads of the carpet. Protected from light, they feed on minute organic debris. After passing some time closed in a resistant cocoon, the larvae evolve into adult fleas, which proceed to jump onto the cat. Thanks to the nourishment provided by the animal's blood, they are then able to lay dozens of new eggs, starting of a

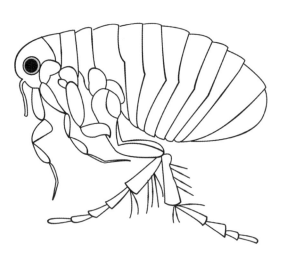

One flea can bite tens of times a day. This is why an infestation causes the animal to scratch and bite itself to the point of causing lesions.

new reproductive cycle. But, how can you tell if your cat has fleas? First of all, by keeping an eye on its behavior: persistent scratching, sudden jerking and biting of the coat should all ring alarm bells, as well as the presence of small black specks (the parasite's feces) on the fur left on the brush during grooming sessions. Unless the cat has a serious infestation or a pure white coat, it will be rather difficult to actually see fleas moving around on the fur.

Once the presence of the parasites has been confirmed, you must intervene immediately because the greatest danger of an infestation is not actually the irritating itching provoked by the bites, but the amount of blood that these insects can drink, which if left unchecked can even trigger anemia, especially in kittens and ill or malnourished subjects. In addition, some cats may develop an intolerance to flea saliva: in such cases, even a very small number of insects is sufficient to trigger extremely itchy skin inflammation, loss of hair and the formation of scabbing in various parts of the body. It should also be remembered that the flea may also be a carrier for another rather common parasite that can infect humans as well, the dipylidium caninum, a tapeworm. It is ingested along with the flea that hosts it during the cat's regular grooming sessions and takes up

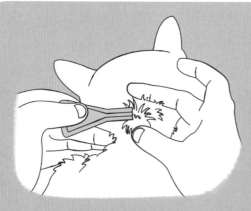

residence in the small intestine triggering irritating itching in the anal area as well as constipation or diarrhea. Then there is the bartonella henselae, the bacteria responsible for what's commonly known as the Cat Scratch Disease or Trench Fever. These bacteria may be present on a cat's claws, where flea feces usually accumulate. Hence, they can be transmitted to humans via scratches, triggering localized infections, which although not dangerous, can be rather irritating.

To effectively combat fleas, you must follow the instructions of your veterinarian as to the best product for your case. There are excellent medicated flea shampoos, collars, drops to apply between the shoulder blades and even pills available on the market. All of these products are effective, but you must carefully follow the instructions provided on the packaging. They should be used only for healthy animals (in proportion to their age and weight) and do not need a vet's prescription. Be especially careful not to use flea treatments formulated for dogs because cats cannot tolerate them. Obviously, the cleanliness of the surrounding environment is also very

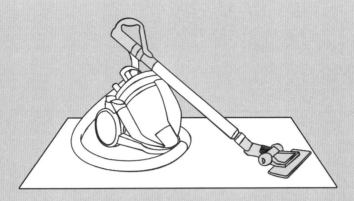

important: after confirming that your cat has fleas and treating it, it is extremely important to use a flea spray to eliminate the larvae as well, to vacuum repeatedly (changing the filter often) and to wash all covers and pillow cases. Steam cleaning is particularly effective, especially on mattresses and pillows.

Ticks, like fleas, feed on the cat's blood. They are not commonly found on indoor cats, but for outdoor cats or those in contact with dogs, the risk is not one to take lightly. When the ticks attach themselves, they bury their rostrum (mouth parts) in the skin and begin to harvest blood, storing it in their body, which can increase in size by as much as 200 times. These insects can be carriers of serious diseases such as Lyme disease, also known as Lyme borreliosis (a bacterial infection that attacks the joints, nervous system, internal organs and the skin). If you find a tick feeding on your cat, extract it being very careful not to leave its head behind: use a pair of blunt-tipped tweezers to take hold of the parasite as close to the skin as possible and twist gently, as if you are removing a bolt. Even if successful, a visit to the veterinarian is still a good idea.

Two Terrifying Diseases

The diseases that a cat can develop are many. Some of them are very serious and incurable to this day. Two of these have become very well known among cat lovers due to the attention they have been given by the media and alarmist word of mouth: feline immunodeficiency virus and feline infective peritonitis. The former, commonly called feline AIDS (not transmissible to humans), is one of the most serious diseases a cat can get because it attacks the immune system, leaving the animal vulnerable to extremely violent infections. The most common infection route is via bites by infected

animals. For this reason, male cats that are free to go outside and brawl with other cats are four times more likely to develop this disease than females. Diagnosis is made following a test but unfortunately, there are no drugs available that can neutralize the virus, although some are being developed. Once contracted, the only way to combat this terrible disease is to treat each infection as it develops.

Another "nightmare" for a cat owner is feline infective peritonitis, also known as FIP. The culprit of this extremely dangerous and highly contagious disease is the feline coronavirus. It can manifest itself in a "wet" form (characterized by the secretion of a thick, yellowish discharge in quantities that can be quite substantial into the stomach, which begins to visibly swell) and a "dry" form (which mainly affects the kidneys and the liver, but also the eyes and more rarely the nervous system, with symptoms that vary from balance problems to seizures). Unfortunately, currently there are few treatments for this disease. One option is to establish a treatment plan focused on alleviating symptoms and providing support to the affected organs. Such a plan can substantially slow disease progression and prolong the animal's life.

Like feline AIDS, the best way to protect our furry friend in this case is prevention. Both of these viruses are transmitted by direct contact with an infected feline: if you note the presence of unregistered cat colonies in your neighborhood, it will be best to avoid allowing the cat to wander away from home.

The Older Cat

Old age is a very delicate time for a cat because its body begins to wear out, its limbs become weaker, the senses become duller and vital organs begin to tire. From the eighth/tenth year of age, the cat's life becomes a bit more complicated due to the inevitable accumulation of problems caused by some typical conditions. The most common of these is without a doubt renal insufficiency, i.e. reduced kidney function, characterized by difficulty in clearing toxins from the body and retaining the liquids needed for proper hydration. It is easily diagnosed, even by the owner, because initial symptoms include increased use of the litter box and excessive drinking, followed by physical exhaustion, loss of appetite and even difficulty in maintaining balance when walking. Cats suffering from this condition,

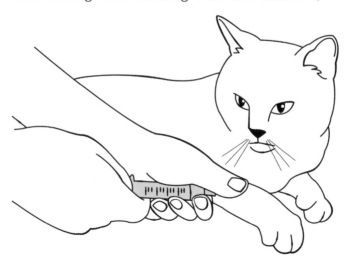

which requires clinical exams to be verified, are treated with a diet low in protein, to decrease the load on the kidneys, but also low in sodium and phosphate, rich in B-group vitamins and with higher fiber contents.

There are different preparation available on the market, both dry and wet, that meet these requirements, which are quite difficult to achieve in a homemade meal. It is also very important to allow the cat access to large quantities of fresh water.

In addition to kidney problems, an old cat is vulnerable to other relatively typical conditions. These include diabetes (reduction in or lack of insulin production by the pancreas which means sugars introduced into the body in foods cannot be utilized by the cells), hyperthyroidism (disruption in the function of the thyroid gland which begins to produce incorrect amounts of hormones), oral cavity diseases and increased risk of tumor development.

Just as for all the elderly, teeth are a sore point for cats as well: since an old animal can lose many teeth and have difficulty chewing, it's best to avoid giving it foods prepared at home, which may have gristle that could be potentially dangerous if swallowed whole. The litter box will also be visited more often. Outdoor cats, on the other hand, may no longer be able to hold in every bodily function long enough to get to their favorite spot in the backyard. Hence, you will need to find an easily accessible spot for a litter box, especially if the cat has arthritis.

5.
Living
Together
Well

To live well with a cat you must learn to think and behave as cats do. It may seem easy to do, but it's not. Recent studies, particularly those by John W. Bradshow of the Anthrozoology Institute of the University of Bristol, have shown that a cat is incapable of establishing a hierarchical relationship based on clearly defined, unique roles with fellow cats or with humans. Unlike dogs, whose practice of hunting in groups has forced them to develop a refined communication system between individuals to ensure the best outcome for the hunt, the cat, who is a solitary hunter, perceives everything around him only in relation to itself. Therefore, while for a dog the owner may somehow come to represent the alpha male of the pack to which it belongs or a member of a community to protect; for a cat, the owner is always another feline to be treated as an equal. This is the key to understanding how stimulating living with a cat can be: every day must be a search for new ways of communicating, which once learned (by you), will become rules to follow to ensure a truly extraordinary life together.

Many helpful tips for a satisfying life together can be extracted from some simple and basic considerations. First of these is that to your cat, its human family is no other but a feline colony composed of itself and other cats. Understanding this will help you realize that the relationship that the cat develops with certain members of the family should never be mistaken for respect, affection or dislike. For example, the cat will tend to play with a child more energetically, just as it would with a young cat, increasing the risk of injury if the game transforms itself into a fight for dominance unbeknownst to the human. To understand this delicate mechanism you must take the time to observe a cat colony. In a colony, each individual lives a completely autonomous life, especially during mealtime, coming into contact with other members only at certain times and exhibiting different behaviors towards different individuals. This is why, for example, yelling or hitting a cat in hopes of making our authority felt does not accomplish anything: a slap on the backside or a scolding will never be perceived as a punishment

The great ecologist Konrad Lorenz wrote, "the cat is an independent creature, who does not consider itself a prisoner but on par with man."

because in a cat colony, there is no alpha male capable of "punishing" or isolating one member of the pack or another. The only way to get results is to break its concentration and distract it from the mischief it is about to do with a loud noise, sudden call (its name) or exclamation that could be perceived by the cat as a clear warning advising it that it's about to violate your territory. The same applies to other important moments including petting sessions with long strokes and strategic scratching of the ears: it is not uncommon to see two cats, who get along well within a cat colony, grooming and petting each other. This explains why many cats will often thank you with a lick as you give them a long stroke and sink your fingers into their fur. Many of the cat's typical behaviors can be explained by this dynamic. For example, its tendency to disappear when there are guests in the house. The introduction of a new member into the colony, with new smells and sounds, must be evaluated with maximum care. Unlike a dog, who greets guests enthusiastically if he sees that the owner is pleased to see them (with the exception of guard dogs, which are selected specifically to exhibit the opposite behavior), the trust expressed by other members of the colony towards a new arrival is not sufficient for a cat.

Behavior Disorders

One often hears talk of behavior disorders in cats. Without negating their existence, it should be specified that often, this term is used inaccurately to refer to behaviors undesirable to humans. Marking of territory by spraying terribly smelling urine on furniture and scratching of the house walls and armchairs, are some of these behaviors. Expecting a cat to behave differently is completely unrealistic: these behaviors, in spite of their unpleasant nature, serve the cat in the wild to signal its presence. Even hyperactivity at night should not be confused for a behavior that needs correcting: cats are nocturnal hunters, hence it's perfectly normal for them to play and run around the house chasing various objects during the night. Another common behavior that

There is always a reason behind a sudden change in behavior. Finding the cause could prove very complicated and may even require the help of a veterinarian.

is often inaccurately confused for a "disorder" is sudden aggression during petting sessions: this is not the thoughtless reaction that it appears to be but a signal meant to let you know that the petting is not wanted. It is no different from a show of aggression that the cat would direct at another cat that has crossed a personal boundary.

This does not mean that atypical behavior cannot present itself in some cats. Such behaviors should be watched closely to avoid them degenerating into problems that can turn serious. There are many examples, but perhaps the most common is performing bodily functions outside the litter box. This does not include spraying, which serves to mark territory, but actual excrements left on carpets, beds or even clothes. If this happens, it means there is something in the house that disturbs the cat: it may be related to the litter box (uncomfortable shape, unpleasantly smelling litter, wrong location) or some smell or noise that no one but the cat can perceive (such as the extremely high-pitched noise emitted by some electrical devices). It is highly unlikely that you are dealing with what is often defined, with "humanocentric" lightness, as "mischief". Once illnesses of the intestine that would prevent the cat from getting to the litter box in time have been

excluded with the help of a veterinarian, all you have to do is perform a careful and thorough search for the cause of cat's discomfort.

Even excessive grooming of the coat or other parts of the body should alarm you because it is a clear sign of stress, which if untreated, can lead to skin inflammation and serious lesions.

The first question you should ask yourself when a cat suddenly changes its behavior is if the cat is trying to send you a message, or get your attention. It is not unusual for a cat to feel its territory threatened due to a change in the daily routine, perhaps due to the arrival of a new partner in the house. Restoring the balance in the emotional atmosphere in such a situation is no less easy, but it is possible one step at a time. For example, if a new roommate has moved into the house, you will obviously have to wait for him/her to become "familiar": what's most important in the initial period is not to force the cat in any way and to wait for it to make the first move and show what it expects from you. You need to try your best to see things, or better yet "smell" things, from the cat's point of view: with

over 200 million olfactory cells, as compared to the barely 5 million in humans, the cat can perceive odors hidden to humans. Hence, there should be no need to explain how much a new odor or aroma brought into the house by a stranger can irritate or even attract a cat. This is why it is best to do things slowly. Before the new arrival moves into your apartment, leave some clothing impregnated with their smell around the house. If the cat is still stressed and scared, a Bach flower remedy may help. This is a natural substance that can be prescribed by the veterinarian, which can help calm and re-equilibrate some behavior disorders, including excessive aggression, which is always a symptom of emotional problems. Recently, a lot of progress has been made in acupuncture. However, it is still always best to consult a veterinarian before undertaking any kind of treatment.

6.
Going on Vacation

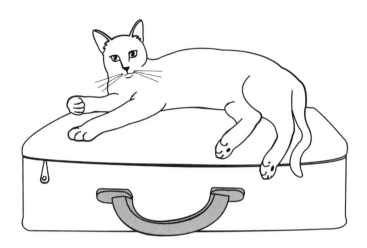

Many cats love traveling and moving with their master even if they are housed in the strangest places, from the basket of a bicycle to a backpack. It is a matter of habit: if from the time they are kittens, they get used to being carried around, as adults, they will have no problem with traveling and will continually adapt to their new accommodation. In principle, it must be said that a cat does not like to give up its household habits and leave their territory unattended.

If we cannot take them with us to the beach or into the mountains, the ideal solution is then to leave them at home in the care of a trusted catsitter that brings them food to eat, cleans the litter and pets them.

If instead, we are not able to bring our cat with us, we have to go to a kennel. It is nonetheless money well spent because the cat will also have the chance to go to the vet. There are several models on the market for transporting cats, but the right one must have some essential characteristics.

First of all it must be made of resistant, non-toxic and washable materials, and be equipped with a system for opening and closing that makes the entry and exit of the cat as smooth as possible. This is necessary to prevent the transport from becoming even more traumatic: the opening should be on the front and as wide as possible so that the cat can be placed inside without being picked up or handled excessively in order to be pushed inside. The ideal material is plastic because it is washable and does not decay or become full of unpleasant odors as often happens with wood or wicker. There are some models which are more open and others that are more closed.

The right choice depends on how intimidated the cat is by new things.

If you plan to travel on vehicles such as trains, planes or ships, you need to also pay attention to the dimensions of the carrier. Many airlines, for example, have regulated standards that are usually around 28

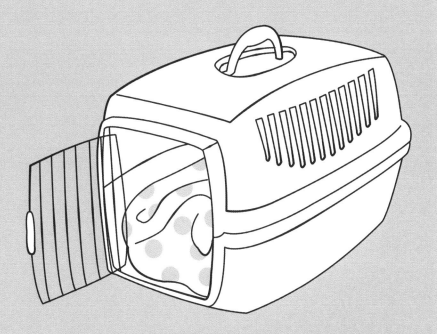

inches long (70 cm) and 12-15 inches wide (30-40 cm) and 20 inches high (50 cm), with a total weight (including the cat) of approximately 23 pounds (10 kg). These are, of course, guidelines which may vary from company to company and from country to country, but they represent an approximate average.

It is not advisable to insert bowls with food and water inside the carrier, as they will likely turn over causing the carrier to become dirty as well as cause discomfort for the animal. Instead, it is useful to insert sheets of newspaper onto the bottom of the carrier to absorb any urine and feces. For trips in which the cat will travel without us, such as those by plane (generally not recommended because of the high degree of stress that is causes), it is useful to leave a garment soaked with our scent to make them feel less alone.

Transportation

The car is without a doubt the most highly recommended means of transport for journeys with cats because, in addition to being less noisy than trains, ships and planes, it allows for stops in case of emergency. However, a carrier is essential. If possible, it is advisable to secure it to the seat using the seat belts. There are some animals that are calm if they can see what is happening outside and others who get panicky in the same situation and prefer isolation and discretion. The only way to discover this is through experience.

If during the trip the cat shows excessive

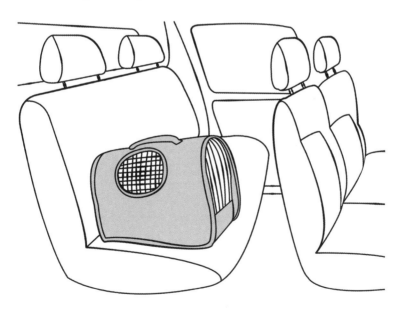

Travelling can represent a major source of stress for a cat. Travel as comfortably as possible, but always respecting the law and the relevant regulations.

impatience by means of prolonged meowing or continuously scraping the sides of the carrier, it would be good to stop for a short time and pet them comfortingly and grant them some delicious tidbit, but always without removing them to avoid any dangerous escapes.

During the summer, it is important to have screens on the car windows to make sure that the sun does not hit the top of the carrier. It is equally important not to keep the air conditioning too high to avoid sudden temperature changes when getting them out of the cabin of the vehicle.

On train, as on buses, regulations require that a cat must travel in a carrier. In this case, it is especially important to act with common sense: if our cat suffers while traveling and as soon as it is placed in the carrier begins to meow incessantly, it would be better not to take them on any means of transport which could annoy the other passengers. If we know that the cat does not tolerate separation from us, it is better to book a seat next to ourselves upon which the carrier can be placed so that we can always see each other. Those who want to travel in a sleeping car with their cat can do so under certain conditions: you must make a reservation in which you specify the

presence of the animal and that the cat will remain closed in the appropriate carrier for the duration of the trip and that the entire compartment has been reserved. The payment of the fee that is charged for the disinfection of the sleeping bunk, to be paid at the time of the booking of the ticket, has instead recently been abolished.

Regardless of the means chosen, in any case, it is always necessary to take clean newspapers with you in case the cat dirties the ones stored on the bottom of the carrier (and also to avoid the spread of embarrassing odors), as well as a small bowl for food and one for water that can be filled during the vehicle's stops. In extreme cases, with a veterinarian's prescription, you can give the animal some tranquillizers to prevent them feeling bad during the journey.

Planes are certainly the least desirable means of transport for your feline friend: in fact, companies rarely allow for the placement of the carrier in the cabin and, therefore, because they are placed in the hold, we have no way to check on the status of the animal. The noises of the motors, pressurization and the tossing around during the operations of loading and unloading can become a source of truly serious trauma that is difficult to remove. Unfortunately, the same thing also applies when travelling by ship.

For trips abroad, in addition to regular vaccinations which must be certified on the health card of the animal (and carried always), the insertion of subcutaneous microchips for all dogs and cats is obligatory, along with the showing of their passport, for some countries such as Korea.

7.
Cat
Messages

The basis of the feline language, even before sounds and smells, is made up of their body language. An arched back and standing up on outstretched legs, for example, is never a good sign: it means that the cat is nervous and it is on the defensive, trying to increase its weight to appear even bigger and intimidate those who are in front of it, often also raising its hair and puffing out its tail into an arch. It is clearly a threat that, in the most common cases, is accompanied by its ears flattening back and opening its mouth with murmurs and growls. This is a rather typical pose of cats that are fighting for control of territory or in the conquest of a female, often taken on by kittens when they are playing (for cats, this is training that is done to understand the mechanisms that regulate fighting and hunting rather than for fun games).

In all of these poses, the ears play a very important role. Moved by a complex muscular system, they are able to rotate 180 degrees and bend, taking on very different positions. When they are pointing forwards and very straight: the cat is at maximum attention watching its surrounding environment, studying everything and listening carefully. When they are bent back and flattened to the sides of the head, they instead symbolize aggression. In this case, the purpose is to focus the attention of the observer on the cat's mouth, which will be open to show their teeth, with their whiskers outstretched forward.

Equally important in the feline "dictionary" is the language of the tail. If a cat meets you in regular passing with its tail straight, perhaps with the tip of the tail a little bit bent to the side as if forming a question mark, it means that you present no aggressive threat, and demonstrates their highest level of openness. This stance makes it possible to show their rear and let another cat (and us) sniff under their tail and displays their availability to be social. Even a super- straight vibrant tail is a positive signal, often used while waiting for us to give them food. It is the simulation of a very similar behavior that cats use when spraying urine on trees and

walls to mark their territory. When they use it near our legs, and rub back and forth, this attitude means that the cat is asserting its ownership of the master. Obviously, we don't need to worry about this gesture unless it becomes associated with the real marking of territory, since it is normally just an "emotional" simulation. Instead, when the cat's tail is down between their legs, just like in a dog, it indicates fear and acquiescence. The coverage of their genitals clearly shows that the animal does not want to interact with the external environment and is seeking protection.

The similarities to dogs disappear if the cat's tail is moved jerkily through the air to the right and left: what may look like the pleasurable wagging of a dog's tail, in feline language, is instead evidence of a nervousness that could turn quickly into aggression. It is no coincidence that this signal is also implemented during playtime, when the emotional state of the cat practices how to attack and ambush. This is one of their classic behaviors that can be completely misunderstood by man, along with lying on their back showing their belly.

In this case it is true that the cat is asking for pampering putting themselves in an obvious position of submission, but it is equally true that, when it is associated with a particular state of nervousness, this behavior can be a defensive strategy that allows the cat to use all four paws to scratch an attacker who attacks from an elevated position. If a cat shows us their belly but has their ears back, whiskers forward and tail moving jerkily, then putting our hand between their legs could prove to be a very bad decision.

Vocal Messages

Anyone who has been in the company of a cat for at least a full day knows: a cat can meow in many different ways. The modulation of the sounds, in fact, plays an important role in feline communication: from a meow to a growl, from a murmur to a purr, there's an entire dictionary of sounds that it is good to learn to understand and translate. Suffice it to say that the scholar Mildred Moelk was able to show that some Siamese cats, the race of cats that is without a doubt the most talkative, are even able to "pronounce" nine consonants and five vowels! Anecdotes aside, we can say that cats use their voice to scare, ask for something and win people over. In the first case, real prolonged yowls modulated at different frequencies, accompanied by guttural growls and murmurs which are used to intimidate the enemy at hand, occur

It's easy to say "meow." A cat meows in different ways to communicate different things: asking for something to eat, looking for a mate or expressing discomfort.

especially when another cat invades their territory or in a duel of love between two males facing off for a female. This type of "yowling" is produced when they are in a state of attention and often reaches its highest point right before the actual attack, as if it were a war cry. Similar to these, acoustically, are the cries of love that male cats emit when they are in heat to attract females and to make their presence felt even hundreds of feet away. Although some sentimentalists define these as "serenades", they actually sound really awkward and seem to be modulated in a long sequence of consonants pronounced entirely by chance. A female in heat usually responds with meows that are much more subdued and acute and accompanied by loud purring that shows their availability for mating.

Then there's the real meow, the most common one, the classic "meow", which can be uttered to ask us for something like food, to attract our attention towards a closed window to be opened, to greet us upon our return home or to signal to us something that is out of the ordinary. If the demand is for food, the meowing will be particularly acute and parceled out, often insistent, and may even be accompanied by a purring sound. Karen McComb, a professor at Sussex University, has conducted research on

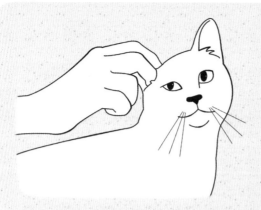

this type of meow classifying it as "manipulative": by observing the reaction of fifty people who were put in front of a cat meowing, she has concluded that these sounds allow the animal to get what he wants by activating the same emotional reaction in our brain that is activated when we hear a child crying. The same involuntary association happens when a sick or injured cat emits a kind of "aw" that is very rhythmic and with which they ask for help by showing pain. Decidedly less disturbing is the affectionate "purr" uttered with their mouth shut and with which the cat is usually thanking their master after an unplanned stroking.

Then there are the classic purrs, the "trilling", or the "purr" as the British call it, that our cat friends use to show complacency and satisfaction. It is a more or less subdued sound, between 25 and 50 Hz, that the cat emits with their mouth closed when they are satisfied, or when trying to calm down after experiencing something very stressful. Although it may seem incredible, we still do not know for sure exactly how this sound is produced: according to some scholars, it is the result of the vibration of some "extra" vocal cords found in the throat, while others would ascribe

it to the regulation of blood flow in the vena cava that resonates while vibrating in the chest. We do know for a fact that its "calming" origins can found in the first days of a cat's life, when kittens begin to make small almost imperceptible purring sounds during feeding to thank their mother for her milk, and which also responds with the same sound. That's why when we caress our cat, we are thanked with auditory purring and with the rhythmic movement of their legs that we like to call "kneading the dough" (an action that kittens apply to the stomach of their mothers to help the milk come out). Not only that, according to some studies conducted in the United States, it seems that cats, when they are purring, generate endorphins, substances that are produced by the brain and which have soothing properties similar to those of morphine and opium. That's probably why cats also purr when they are sick or shortly before their death.

Scent Messages

Powered by 200 million olfactory cells, a cat's nose is an amazing machine that can sense odors even at long distances and analyze them with great skill. With a simple "sniff of their nose", a cat is entirely capable of sensing the presence of a living being within hundreds of feet from them without seeing them and is able to identify their traces in order to follow them or run away. In this way, communication by "smelling" makes up a crucial aspect of the feline world, equal to sound and vision as means of communication.

Many people know all too well the pungent and unpleasant smell of spraying that males, especially those which are not neutered, use to indicate their territory by spraying urine on trees and walls. However, few know that when a cat rubs their cheeks or mouth insistently on our pants, on our shoes or on the

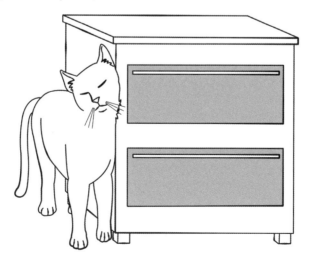

edges of the furniture, it does so to leave odorous markings. Fortunately, they are only barely perceptible traces for refined noses like that of a cat, markings that are issued by the sebaceous glands located below their cheeks, chin and neck that secrete substances (called pheromones) containing all the information about who left them. Thanks to the so-called vomeronasal organ (also called Jacobson's organ), placed on their palate, the cat is able to move the air inhaled into their mouth towards their olfactory receptors, which in turn send it to the brain to be analyzed. When this sophisticated perceptual system is activated by moving the cat's head upwards and keeping their mouth slightly open, with rapid movements of the tongue that favor the passage of air onto the palate, it is said that the cat applies "flehmen" (from the German verb "flehmen" that indicates the very act of showing the upper row of the teeth).

It is also important to debunk the myth about smells that a neutered or spayed cat no longer produces. Instead, it is quite common that a sterilized cat also emits a bitter, pungent, nauseating odor due to the secretions of the so-called "anal glands". These are organs which are located in the area of the anus that are responsible for secreting substances that leave a "personal" smell on a cat's stool that is used by other cats passing by to "identify" the owner of that territory. It can however occur that these substances are released unintentionally, most likely due to a particular state of excitement or to an inflammation of the glands which release a terrible odor into the environment that can only be removed by cleaning well with soapy water.

8.
Cats with a Pedigree

Although there are more than fifty cat breeds recognized by the major cat associations today, the concept of breed in the world of cats has a relatively recent history. In 1871, at the Crystal Palace in London, under the patronage of Queen Victoria, the first cat show was held, having been organized by Harrison Weir. On this occasion, all of the breeds then known came to England: the magnificent Angoras from the East, the new Persians obtained by cross-breeding them with the most robust English cats, the charming cats with sapphire eyes raised by the King of Siam, the refined blue cats loved by the Russian nobles and some giant cats coming from the North. It was the official entrance of the cat in the Hall of pure-bred animals, a title that before had only been awarded to dogs (particularly hunting dogs).

But how is a breed born? First, it is worth pointing out that there are "natural" breeds and those that are "obtained". The first case refers to cats with certain physical characteristics that have occurred because of spontaneous adaptation to their surrounding environment (such as the long-hair and large-size of Nordic cats), whereas the latter is produced by human intervention through long selective processes aimed at achieving a well-defined aesthetic purpose (such as a specific color or a specific shape of the ears). In both cases, the first step in the creation (or preservation) of a breed is the genetic isolation of the physical characteristics (as well as those of character) that will become and remain proprietary. Once these have been "stabilized", through targeted cross-breeding and selection, the application of the so-called standard proceeds: the identification of a series of mandatory features that every cat should possess. Then it can be included in the foundation of the so-called "club of breeds", that is, the institution that will monitor the purity of the breed and the adherence to the standards by being associated with and coordinating

with specialized breeders. The official recognition of a breed, which can take tens of years of work, must be proposed by the club of breeds and sanctioned by the feline associations. The major international associations to be mentioned are the WCF (World Cat Federation), the CFA (Cat Fanciers Association), the FIFé (Fédération Internationale Féline) and the TICA (The International Cat Association). FIFé (Fédération Internationale Féline) "catalogs" cat breeds into four categories: the 2nd and 3rd categories were established by the length of the hair (medium-long or short); and the 1st and 4th according to the body structure of the cat ("Persian" and "Eastern" type).

Natural Breeds

Among the many breeds that are now officially recognized, few boast the title "natural", that is, a breed selected from nature without any human intervention. Of these, one can mention especially the Nordic cats, which have developed in inhospitable and isolated environments. First of all, there is the Siberian, a Russian cat whose coat has a mane and characteristic tufts on its ears which are the legacy of a habitat with very low temperatures. Actually the low level of human intervention on this breed is due to the difficulty of exporting (and importing) animals from the Soviet Union before the fall of the Berlin Wall that has preserved the breeds from the Western tendency to change the features of wild cats in order to adapt to the whims of fashion. The Norwegian Forest and Maine Coon cats, two other Nordic breeds of considerable size, can claim

There is a breed for everyone. Some are the result of the whims of Mother Nature, while others are the result of decades of careful selection by geneticists and breeders.

the title of "natural". Unlike their Russian cousins, however, the hand of man has begun to leave obvious signs mainly due to the reckless rush towards their giant size. Although huge cats are already spoken about in ancient legends, cats that were so powerful that they could not even be lifted by strong Odin, the Norwegian cats of today are certainly much more massive than they were years ago.

Even the Abyssinian, with ancient origins coming from Africa, can be considered a natural breed, along with the spotted Egyptian Mau which comes from the same area. In both cases, the hallmarks of cats depicted by the ancient Egyptians thousands of years ago can be recognized almost intact. In these two cases, in fact, man has limited itself to preserving the specific characteristics of the two races in order to avoid them being lost as a result of interbreeding with European cats. This refers specifically to the "ticking" of the Abyssinian (the characteristic color of the coat due to the alternation of colored bands on every single hair) and the dark spots of the Egyptian Mau. Unfortunately this does not apply to Somali cats, the long-haired version of the Abyssinian obtained by breeders through a series of targeted cross-breeding. Even the Turkish Angora, imported to Europe from Turkey by Italian travelers in the 17th century, is a natural breed.

How the Breeds Are Created

There are many cases in which common cats born with a "defect" have attracted the attention of some breeder suggesting the identification of a new breed. This is the case of the Sphynx, the famous hairless cat that owes its appearance to a trivial, accidental genetic mutation that has been masterfully isolated and preserved by man. This is similar to the case which led to the recognition of other particularly furry breeds such as the Rex (Devon Rex, Cornish Rex, Selkirk Rex, German Rex), all characterized by uniquely curly fur which occurred randomly because of some genetic mutation that is today controlled and produced by skilled breeders. The path towards the selection of

The Persian has always been one of the most popular breeds, but lately its popularity has been challenged by breeds like the Maine Coon or the Norwegian Forest cat.

a breed is long and requires continuous experiments to understand how a specific feature can be transmitted to kittens, practicing cross-breeding between cats with similar characteristics, but also very different ones in order not to deplete the blood lines with too many cases of inbreeding. This age-old process of selection, moving back and forth between bureaucracy, veterinary practices and genetics, was also used by the breeders of the American Curl and the Scottish Fold, two breeds that have unusual folding of their ears as their peculiar characteristic, towards the back in the first case and towards the front in the second. Rather original, however, is the case of the Ragdoll, American cats that go limp when they are picked up by the arms of their master. It is said that the progenitor of the breed was beautiful Josephine, a cat that was hit by a car and upon which the University of California performed top-secret genetic testing. But the true story is rather different: breeders of Ragdoll cats, starting from Josephine, who had the unusual habit of going completely limp when she was picked up, tried to isolate the peculiarities of the cat's character rather than physical ones, starting from kittens who clearly demonstrated the same behavior. Many breeds have also been "created" by man by breeding starting practically from nothing.

One of these is the Toyger, a very recent breed, whose creation came about only because of the work with a group of breeders who wanted to create a domestic cat that resembles a tiger in every way. Even the Siamese cat as we know it today was obtained "in a laboratory": it came from the East, from the Kingdom of Siam after which they take their name, but the first examples of the breed were not as slender and "triangular" as those of today.

This goal was reached after years of work: the desire was to "create" an animal that had in its "design" the elegance of the cats depicted in ancient Oriental prints. The desire of some breeders to recreate the ancient Siamese cat led in turn to the recognition of a breed called Thai cats. Just as the increasingly frequent birth of Siamese cats without the characteristic darker color on their tail, face, ears and legs brought about the identification of the Oriental breed (solid-colored Siamese cats). We can also include Persians in this category, the only cat that can boast the title "long-haired" (with a record long coat that can be as long as 8 inches [20 cm]), unlike all the other breeds that have to settle for "medium-long".

In this case, the selection process started for the express purpose of obtaining a coat for its softness and length: it took almost a hundred years and thousands of cross-breeding attempts between Turkish Angora cats, smaller cats from Persia and British Shorthair cats (a large robust one hundred per cent English cat) to reach the result that is seen today with their distinctive flattened muzzle that is much-loved by their admirers (there is also a short-haired version know as Exotic Persian). Looking towards the future, we can say that the newest breeds of cats are becoming really extraordinary, those that are still in the process of selection but that in a few decades will be ready to be approved as a breed in every respect. These are known as "hybrids", big cats obtained by cross-breeding domestic cats with wild cats of Asian or African origins. Of these, it is worth mentioning the Chausie (obtained by crossing Abyssinians, Orientals, and Bengals with specimens of *Felis chaus*, an Asian big cat known as the Jungle Cat), the large Savannah cats (a cross between domestic spotted cats and the *Leopardus geoffroyi*) or the great Savannah (descending from Serval cats, African felines of medium to large

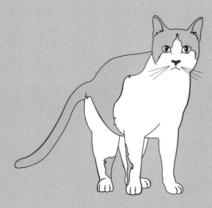

size from the southern Sahara). Other hybrids which are still completing their genetic development are the Desert Lynx (obtained by cross-breeding between small wild short-tailed lynxes), the Caracat (a cross between Abyssinian and Caracal cats), the Jambi (a cross-breeding of the *Prionailurus viverrinus* which is known as the Fishing Cat), the Cheetoh (a cross between Ocelot and Bengal cats) and the Habari (a cross between Jungle and Bengal cats). As for the origin of the names of the breeds, they often recall the source of the first examples of the breed, perhaps combined with a word that summarizes their look. This is the case of the Scottish Fold (because of the bending forward of their ears), the American Curl (because of the curl formed by the ears bent backwards), the Japanese Bobtail (with their tails cut in Japanese style), the Siamese (from the ancient kingdom of Siam) and Birman cats (which according to legend was imported to England by some British travelers return from the kingdom of Burma). The European cat, often called the "common cat" or "mestizo" (it is instead a very specific breed recognized by the International Feline Federation Feline in 1982), is also called a

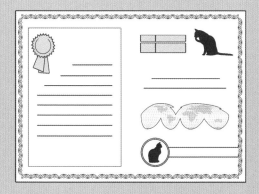

"Tabby." Some people instead give in to their imagination inventing slightly more unique names, as happened for the Munchkin, whose name recalls that of the dwarves that appear in the film "The Wizard of Oz." If you decide to buy a purebred cat, you need to be sure that the sellers give you the pedigree. It is a document, a kind of identity card, which certifies the registration of the cat in the Register of Origins (a sort of official feline registry) of a specific Feline Association. It contains all the information about the cat (name, sex, date of birth, color and registration number), the manifest (that is the name of the breeder where it was born, accompanied by the information and address of the breeder) and references to its brothers and sisters from the same litter all of its ancestors for the previous four or five generations. This information allows the association to certify that the cat is descended from specimens of pure breed (each with their own pedigree) and can therefore participate in competitions and shows. It should, in fact, be noted that a cat without a pedigree, even if it perfectly corresponds to all the canons of the breed to which it belongs, can never be considered purebred.

9.
Becoming a Mother

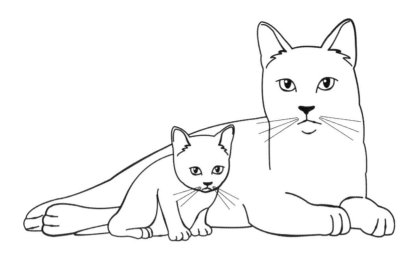

If we decide not to sterilize our cat, the terms "heat", "mating", "pregnancy" and "birth" will become part of our everyday vocabulary, whether we like it or not. That's why it is important to understand their meaning well.

Let's start with "heat". Scientifically called "oestrus", it defines those particular times during the year when the cat declares itself to available for mating by emitting meowing sounds and releasing pheromones into the air. The latter, secreted by certain glands (located, for example, on the chin, cheeks, lips and legs), are odorous substances that help to attract males (which are fertile throughout the year and always active). Cats "mark" their territory by spraying the area with urine and feces that also contain pheromones.

The period of heat can be of variable length and is impossible to plan because it depends on many different factors such as the state of health, age, race and even the increase or decrease of daylight hours.

Cats can actually have an unknown number of periods of heat during the eight/nine ideal months from spring to fall.

The first period of heat occurs when the cat reaches sexual maturity, more or less around the sixth month of age, although much depends on the conditions of their life and breed, since, for example, house cats generally tend to mature later, as do long-haired cats. Preceded by a so-called "pre-heat" period, namely a preparatory phase that may last two or three days when the cat generally changes behavior or acts particularly docile and cuddly, or conversely more aggressive and bad-tempered, the heat period is announced by acute meows which are used to attract males, continuous rubbing against things and typical postures, such as an arched back, a raised rear-end

The right age for a first pregnancy is after the cat is 10-11 months old for most breeds. For the Main Coon and Persian breeds, it is best to wait until the cat is 18 months old.

and their tail held to the side. If mating occurs, the period of heat immediately ends, otherwise it can go on for months with long pauses called "anoestrus".

It is important to know that during heat, cats will not menstruate: cats only ovulate if they are given the opportunity to mate, unlike female dogs which ovulate every six months and have the related menstruation.

In all of this, what can we as their masters do? How should we behave?

First of all, if we decide not to sterilize our cat friend, we have to surrender ourselves to the idea that we have to live with this calendar and, if we do not want unwanted kittens, we have to learn to recognize the "dangerous" moments and to close the cat in the house, otherwise it will be almost impossible to keep them away from males that could come from the neighboring balconies or courtyards of the area. That's why the choice of sterilization should be taken with great responsibility: it is better to undergo the small inconvenience of a simple operation that has no moral implications, rather than let the cat go through life without sexual fulfillment which in the long term could cause serious diseases and may result in sleepless nights spent keeping howling male cats away from under windows and having equally noisy scuffles between themselves.

Pregnancy

A cat which is expecting kittens is able to throw the lives of an entire family into turmoil. It is good to remember that this is an ordinary event that an expectant mother, unless there are complications, can handle autonomously by relying on its instincts. Let's have a look at the key stages of pregnancy and find out what we can really do to help our friend.

The pregnancy of a cat, from conception to birth, lasts on average sixty-five days, but the first visible signs appear as early as the seventeenth day, when the cat's nipples become enlarged and their belly begins to swell accompanied by a gradual increase in weight. In this phase, only a veterinarian is able to confirm the actual state of the expectant mother with a palpation of the abdomen and possibly an ultrasound (useless before the fifteenth day). Those who want to avoid eventual disappointment can

also perform an X-ray to make sure there are no malformed kittens: nonetheless, they will have to wait until the fortieth day of pregnancy, since it is around this time that the fetal skeletons begin to be visible. Once it has been established that the cat is pregnant, and we have agreed what to do with the vet, we must try to minimize dangers to the cat, perhaps even preventing them from going out in the garden, where they might hurt themselves or get into a struggle with stray cats, especially during the final fifteen days of the pregnancy. This is actually the most delicate period, during which the animal begins to prepare itself for childbirth and seeks out an appropriate place. In this regard, the advice is to try to figure out which corner of the house seems to catch the cat's attention and follow their choice by equipping it with a warm blanket and freeing it from clothing or materials that could be damaged, stained or cause injuries to the unborn kittens. During the pregnancy, the nutrition of the expectant mother is very important, since a balanced diet will help her stay healthy and ensure the proper development of fetuses. We shouldn't try to become dieticians ourselves, but should rather put our trust in foods that are specifically prepared for pregnant cats and that have been prescribed by a veterinarian. During the first six weeks, we must be careful that the mother does not experience any abrupt changes in weight by guaranteeing their usual daily dose of food, though perhaps increasing it slightly. During the last few weeks, instead, we must fulfill their energy needs by increasing the amount of food by up to 40 per cent. In the final days of the pregnancy, it is important to give the cat small portions of food many times per day.

Birth

If the pregnancy has progressed regularly, any point after the sixty-day time will be the right one for the big event. It is not always easy to see that a cat is in labor, but we can try to pay attention to some changes in behavior such as restlessness and the frenzied search for a sheltered place, together with a drop in body temperature (from 101.3 to 99.5 °F [38.5-37.5 °C]), as well as repeated licking of the area under the tail and a decreased appetite.

Once they have found the right place, and have

Mating is not always successful. Infertility and the interruption of a pregnancy because of a natural abortion are relatively common in cats.

laid down on their side, the cat waits for the start of childbirth: after a series of contractions that can be seen under the tail, a dark bubble will appear. When the first fetus has been completely expelled, followed by the placenta, the mother will rush to lick it vigorously to remove the amniotic fluid and stimulate breathing and circulation. Then it is time for the umbilical cord, which is cut by the mother using their teeth about one inch from the belly of the kitten. If the child birth suddenly stops, do not worry, as there may be a break that could last for a few hours. Attention: particularly if the cat is having its first birth, it is possible that, as a result of experiencing pain, they do not take care of the first kitten. In this case you will have to intervene personally by freeing the snout from the fetal membranes with a sterile gauze. If the umbilical cord doesn't break off by itself, we will have to do it using a lace and a pair of sterilized scissors. Thoroughly clean the body of the little kitten using clean gauze: a massage with a wool rag will help the kitten by stimulating autonomous breathing. These operations are simple but panic and inexperience could make them very complex, which is why it is always good if a veterinarian is present during childbirth. It should be said, however, that serious situations that require the direct intervention

of a veterinarian are rather rare. These include a fetus that is too big or that is suffering from birth defects, the presence of hips that are too narrow (which typical occurs when cats mate too young) or outcomes of fractures, torsion or rupture of the uterus, the absence or insufficiency of contractions (known as uterine inertia, an event more common in cats of advanced age, in those having their first childbirth who are already five years old or have debilitating diseases).

Returning to regular childbirth. From the birth of the first kitten to the next may pass from a few minutes to an hour, for a total of time for childbirth that could be between two and six hours, keeping in mind that the average number of kittens is four (with a maximum of nineteen recorded in medical literature). It is absolutely normal for the mother to eat the placentas that have been expelled because they are rich in nutrients that help them recover from the severe stress of childbirth, but it is important to count them to make sure that none

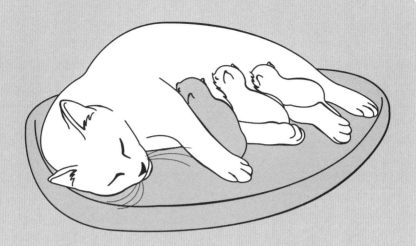

remain inside the uterus and cause infection. The temptation to cuddle those tender little kittens that are about a pound is overwhelming, but we must not give in to sentimentality. The first days of life are extremely delicate for the newcomers and a mother cat will not want to see their kittens taken away from her care, because they are very fragile creatures, still blind (they open their eyes between the tenth and the fourteenth day) and without the immune system that will come from the colostrum, the first milk. The weight of the kittens will increase very rapidly, doubling in the first week. After each meal, the mother licks the body of kittens, with particular focus on the anogenital region. The consumption of meals, along with stimulation from the mother's tongue, causes kittens to make urine and feces, which are eaten by the cat. After giving birth, the new mother will immediately lose 40 per cent of the excess weight gained during pregnancy; the remaining 60 per cent will be disposed of gradually during lactation.

ENRICO ERCOLE, a cat enthusiast, he has been living with cats for his entire life. Since 2005, he has been writing for the most important Italian magazines for cat lovers. He also created a number of special issues dedicated to cat breeds. Among his books, are "I gatti a pelo lungo e semilungo" (Longhair and Medium Hair Cats), "I gatti a pelo corto" (Shorthair Cats) and "I gatti: le razze più rare" (Rarest Cat Breeds). He is the curator of "Gattoni animati", an exhibition about cats in cartoons that took place in WOW Spazio Fumetto – Comics Museum, Milan.

MARISA VESTITA studied painting at the Academy of Fine Arts of Lecce and at the same time she did internships in comics, stage design and stage-craft. Always curious about everything regarding the world of images, in 2002 she moved to Milan where she received her first commissions as an illustrator. She is very interested in applying computer technology to art and completed a course in digital graphic design at the IED (European Institute of Design). She shows in major exhibitions throughout Italy. To date, she collaborated with major Italian publishing houses and magazines, including White Star Kids.

WHITE STAR PUBLISHERS

WS White Star Publishers® is a registered trademark property of De Agostini Libri S.p.A.

© 2016 De Agostini Libri S.p.A.
Via G. da Verrazano, 15 - 28100 Novara, Italy - www.whitestar.it - www.deagostini.it

Translation: TperTradurre

ISBN 978-88-544-1033-6
1 2 3 4 5 6   20 19 18 17 16

Printed in Croatia